spice
DREAMS

Also by Sara Engram and Katie Luber

The Spice Kitchen: Everyday Cooking with Organic Spices

spice
DREAMS

flavored ice creams and
other frozen treats

SARA ENGRAM and KATIE LUBER

with Nancy Meadows and Kimberly Toqe

**Andrews McMeel
Publishing, LLC**

Kansas City • Sydney • London

10 11 12 13 14 WKT 10 9 8 7 6 5 4 3 2 1

ISBN-13: 978-0-7407-8016-5
ISBN-10: 0-7407-8016-6

Library of Congress Control Number: 2009939471

Photography © Maren Caruso Photography (www.marencaruso.com)

Photography: Maren Caruso
Photography assistant: Stacy Ventura
Photography intern: Juliette Tinnus
Food stylist: Kim Kissling
Food stylist assistant: Sarah Fairhurst
Prop stylist: Nissa Quanstrom
Design: Julie Barnes

www.andrewsmcmeel.com

www.tspspices.com
www.smart-spice.com

ATTENTION: SCHOOLS AND BUSINESSES
Andrews McMeel books are available at quantity discounts with bulk purchase for educational, business, or sales promotional use. For information, please write to: Special Sales Department, Andrews McMeel Publishing, LLC, 1130 Walnut Street, Kansas City, Missouri 64106.

To Drew and Betsy Jiranek, for wise counsel and unwavering support, and to the Seasoned Palate team: John Dearing, Tom Shumaker, Bob Grose, Stephanie Adler, Amy Carey, Rosemary Connolly Gately, Lisa Keenan, Moira Eick, Maddie Grose, Jacob Luber, Diana Luber, John Henry Reilly, Jack Dearing, Elizabeth Dearing, Phil Luber, and Jack Reilly.

ICE CREAM. Even the name carries the promise of magic and delight. Whether you lick a cone or savor a spoonful, ice cream has a gift for surprising the palate in the most satisfying of ways. No doubt that's why ice cream comes in almost every flavor imaginable and still continues to inspire adventurous cooks. In this book, we aim to add to the variety in our own favorite way—with top-quality, vibrantly flavored, organic spices.

Spices have always brought a sense of adventure to food, allowing us to imagine ourselves in far-flung places simply by changing the seasonings in a home-cooked meal. Spices can turn a kitchen into the most globally connected room in the house, creating a culinary window on cultures around the world.

We sell and use organic spices because the organic designation provides assurance that spices and herbs are just that—pure spices and herbs without added ingredients such as anticaking agents or extraneous matter like stray stems or twigs. ("Foreign matter" is not tightly regulated for conventional spices.) Pure product means pure flavor, and we're big on flavor.

The recipes in this book rely almost entirely on dried herbs and spices for the simple reason that they are readily available throughout the year. Occasionally, a recipe calls for a fresh herb, as in Basil Ice Cream (page 9). If you don't have a fresh herb available, you can substitute a teaspoon or two of dried for each tablespoon of fresh. If you do have the fresh herb, feel free to supplement the recipe with a teaspoon of dried as well. Using both will provide an extra depth of flavor, intensifying the taste.

Basil ice cream may be new to you, and if it is you have a sweet surprise in store. If you try this recipe—and we hope you will—you may be inspired to experiment with other herbs as well. The same goes for such recipes as Dark Chocolate–Anise Ice Cream (page 24), where fennel seed, or cloves, or some other spice would work equally well. For Mango Sorbet with Cumin and Cinnamon (page 37), you could easily pair allspice and anise seed or use allspice alone.

We have a simple guideline when it comes to spices—suit yourself! In fact, we encourage you to look at these recipes as templates, suggestions for flavor combinations that might surprise and delight your inner ice-cream avatar. A good part of the fun

of homemade ice cream is tweaking these formulas to your own spice preference.

There is some genuinely good commercial ice cream on the market, but nothing quite beats the thrill of tasting the homemade stuff. These days, with handy electric countertop appliances, making ice cream is easier than ever. And, of course, it's still more than worth the effort. When it comes to guilty pleasures, ice cream may be the hardest to resist. Yet somehow, when you take the trouble to make your own, it's hard to feel any guilt at all.

When we went into the spice business, our friend and early colleague, Nancy Meadows, posed a great idea: spiced-up ice cream, or "spice cream." Nancy's skill and imagination produced so many "spice cream" wonders that we were persuaded that ice-cream lovers had a lot of incredibly rewarding new territory to explore. Many of these recipes are straight from Nancy's repertoire. Others have been modified to standardize the recipes and, in some cases, to simplify them to encourage frequent use. For that we turned to our talented friend and culinary expert Kimberly Toqe, who seems able to make every recipe user-friendly.

For all of us at The Seasoned Palate, Inc., the past few months have involved the weighty (alas, we mean that literally) work of making and tasting many different ice creams. We have spared you some (such as green pea sorbet). Others we are delighted to share.

Like most people, we have fond memories of ice cream. Ours reach back to childhood and those backyard sessions with relatives and friends wresting with hand-cranked, and often cranky, ice-enveloped canisters that seemed to take forever to turn custard into ice cream. Even then, the work involved in homemade ice cream was worth the effort.

It's still worth the effort. There's something inherently joyful about eating ice cream—and about making it, too. We find that stirring the custard, which could seem slow and laborious, is a great way to relax and go with the flow—knowing, of course, that the process will yield cold comforts and creamy delights.

Sara and Katie

a few tips:

All ice creams and sorbets should be chilled to 40°F or less before placing in the ice-cream maker. Otherwise, your ice-cream machine will lose its chill too soon and your custard or sorbet will never get firm.

Ice cream calls for egg yolks, but don't waste those egg whites. You can place them in an ice cube tray, one compartment per egg white, and freeze them for later use. Once they're frozen, you can store them in a resealable freezer bag.

Whisking some sugar into the egg yolks helps prevent curdling when tempering. If some of the egg yolks happen to curdle anyway, you can usually rescue the custard by straining the mixture through a fine-mesh sieve before cooling.

Egg custards should be heated to a minimum of 165°F to kill harmful bacteria. These ice-cream recipes call for scalding the milk, which means heating it to just below the boiling point (between 165° and 212°F).

| ice creams |

I scream, you scream—you know the rhyme. Ice cream is one of life's great pleasures. The recipes in this chapter use a common technique, a custard made with milk, cream, sugar, eggs, and seasonings. It's the seasonings that distinguish these recipes.

In our opinion, there's nothing "plain" about a well-made vanilla ice cream, nor anything boring about a simple chocolate or strawberry ice cream. But if that's all you ever get, life can be pretty dull. It's often said that variety is the spice of life, and we happen to think life should be spicy.

In fact, we think full-flavored spices bring a lot of appeal to good, homemade ice cream, opening a brand-new world of delightful taste adventures. Once you taste what a dose of good-quality cardamom or ginger or fennel or anise seed can bring to ice cream, we think you'll find many more reasons to create your own combinations of flavors.

quick and simple spice cream

MAKES 1 PINT *Here's the easiest spice cream of all. Even easier: Serve yourself a bowl of vanilla ice cream and sprinkle cardamom or another favorite spice over it. Enjoy!*

1 pint of your favorite ice cream, slightly softened

1 teaspoon of your favorite spice

Mix together the ice cream and the spice in a medium bowl. Return the ice cream to the original container and freeze for at least 4 hours or overnight.

FLAVOR COMBINATIONS

vanilla and cardamom

chocolate and cloves

strawberry and allspice

vanilla ice cream

MAKES ABOUT 1½ QUARTS *This lemon-laced recipe is a delicious ice cream, but it's also the base for as many enticing variations as your imagination can produce. Try adding 1 to 2 teaspoons of your favorite spice to create your own flavorful spice cream variation.*

2 cups whole milk

½ cup plus ½ cup sugar

1 to 2 teaspoons dried lemon zest

⅛ teaspoon salt

4 large egg yolks

2 cups whipping cream

1 teaspoon vanilla

Combine the milk, ½ cup of the sugar, the lemon zest, and salt in a medium, heavy saucepan. Scald the milk mixture over medium-high heat, stirring often, for 5 minutes.

While the milk is scalding, whisk together the egg yolks in a medium mixing bowl. Add the remaining ½ cup of sugar and whisk until the eggs are light and fluffy. Whisking constantly, add a small amount of the hot milk to the egg mixture. Gradually whisk in the remaining hot milk.

Return the custard mixture to the pan and cook over medium-low heat, stirring often, until the custard is thick enough to coat the back of a spoon, about 5 minutes (see the photo on page xii). Remove the pan from the heat and place in a bowl of ice water to quickly cool the custard. Let the custard cool, stirring often, for 5 minutes.

While the custard is cooling, combine the cream and the vanilla in a medium bowl. Stir in the custard mixture. Cover with plastic wrap and press the wrap directly onto the surface of the custard. Refrigerate until completely chilled, at least 4 hours or overnight. The custard may be stored in the refrigerator for up to 3 days.

Freeze the chilled custard mixture in an ice-cream maker according to the manufacturer's instructions. Transfer the ice cream to an airtight container and freeze in the freezer for 2 to 4 hours before serving.

vanilla-cardamom ice cream

MAKES ABOUT 1½ QUARTS *If you're new to spice cream, this gentle elaboration of good old vanilla is a good place to start. Once you taste the elegance of cardamom-laced ice cream, you'll appreciate what perfect partners ice cream and spices can be. We prefer 2 teaspoons of cardamom in this recipe, but you may want to start with 1.*

2 cups whole milk

½ cup plus ½ cup sugar

1 to 2 teaspoons ground cardamom

⅛ teaspoon salt

4 large egg yolks

2 cups whipping cream

1 teaspoon vanilla

Combine the milk, ½ cup of the sugar, the cardamom, and the salt in a medium, heavy saucepan. Scald the milk mixture over medium-high heat, stirring often, for 5 minutes.

While the milk is scalding, whisk together the egg yolks in a medium mixing bowl. Add the remaining ½ cup of sugar and whisk until the eggs are light and fluffy. Whisking constantly, add a small amount of the hot milk to the egg mixture. Gradually whisk in the remaining hot milk.

Return the custard mixture to the pan and cook over medium-low heat, stirring often, until the custard is thick enough to coat the back of a spoon, about 5 minutes. Remove the pan from the heat and place in a bowl of ice water to quickly cool the custard. Let the custard cool, stirring often, for 5 minutes.

While the custard is cooling, combine the cream and the vanilla in a medium bowl. Stir in the custard mixture. Cover with plastic wrap and press the wrap directly onto the surface of the custard. Refrigerate until completely chilled, at least 4 hours or overnight. The custard may be stored in the refrigerator for up to 3 days.

Freeze the chilled custard mixture in an ice-cream maker according to the manufacturer's instructions. Transfer the ice cream to an airtight container and freeze in the freezer for 2 to 4 hours before serving.

cardamom-mint ice cream

MAKES ABOUT 1½ QUARTS *A teaspoon of mint extract lends an extra tingle to this cardamom-flavored ice cream. These flavors are especially good on a warm summer day. For a fun variation, add ¾ cup of mini semisweet chocolate chips during the last 5 minutes of mixing in the ice-cream maker, for Cardamom–Mint Chip Ice Cream.*

2 cups whole milk

½ cup plus ½ cup sugar

1 to 2 teaspoons ground cardamom

⅛ teaspoon salt

4 large egg yolks

2 cups whipping cream

1 teaspoon vanilla

1 teaspoon peppermint extract

Combine the milk, ½ cup of the sugar, the cardamom, and the salt in a medium, heavy saucepan. Scald the milk mixture over medium-high heat, stirring often, for 5 minutes.

While the milk is scalding, whisk together the egg yolks in a medium mixing bowl. Add the remaining ½ cup of sugar and whisk until the eggs are light and fluffy. Whisking constantly, add a small amount of the hot milk to the egg mixture. Gradually whisk in the remaining hot milk.

Return the custard mixture to the pan and cook over medium-low heat, stirring often, until the custard is thick enough to coat the back of a spoon, about 5 minutes. Remove the pan from the heat and place in a bowl of ice water to quickly cool the custard. Let the custard cool, stirring often, for 5 minutes.

While the custard is cooling, combine the cream, vanilla, and peppermint in a medium bowl. Stir in the custard mixture. Cover with plastic wrap and press the wrap directly onto the surface of the custard. Refrigerate until completely chilled, at least 4 hours or overnight. The custard may be stored in the refrigerator for up to 3 days.

Freeze the chilled custard mixture in an ice-cream maker according to the manufacturer's instructions. Transfer the ice cream to an airtight container and freeze in the freezer for 2 to 4 hours before serving.

orange-nutmeg ice cream

MAKES ABOUT 1½ QUARTS *Nutmeg, coriander, and orange zest blend with all the flair of an accomplished vocal trio. The spices lend interest to this ice cream without overwhelming it. Pair this treat with a Chocolate-Walnut Cookie (page 51) or serve it in a coriander-spiced cone or bowl (page 75) for a delightfully memorable dessert.*

1½ cups whole milk

¼ cup plus ½ cup sugar

2 teaspoons dried orange zest

1 teaspoon ground nutmeg

1 teaspoon ground coriander

⅛ teaspoon salt

4 large egg yolks

2 cups whipping cream

½ cup freshly squeezed orange juice

1 teaspoon vanilla

Combine the milk, ¼ cup of the sugar, the orange zest, nutmeg, coriander, and salt in a medium, heavy saucepan. Scald the milk mixture over medium-high heat, stirring often, for 5 minutes.

While the milk is scalding, whisk together the egg yolks in a medium mixing bowl. Add the remaining ½ cup of sugar and whisk until the eggs are light and fluffy. Whisking constantly, add a small amount of the hot milk to the egg mixture. Gradually whisk in the remaining hot milk.

Return the custard mixture to the pan and cook over medium-low heat, stirring often, until the custard is thick enough to coat the back of a spoon, about 5 minutes. Remove the pan from the heat and place in a bowl of ice water to quickly cool the custard. Let the custard cool, stirring often, for 5 minutes.

While the custard is cooling, combine the cream, orange juice, and vanilla in a medium bowl. Stir in the custard mixture. Cover with plastic wrap and press the wrap directly onto the surface of the custard. Refrigerate until completely chilled, at least 4 hours or overnight. The custard may be stored in the refrigerator for up to 3 days.

Freeze the chilled custard mixture in an ice-cream maker according to the manufacturer's instructions. Transfer the ice cream to an airtight container and freeze in the freezer for 2 to 4 hours before serving.

honey-mint ice cream with thyme and basil

MAKES ABOUT 1½ QUARTS *Sweetened with honey, this herb-flavored ice cream will conjure up the sultry pleasures of a summer day, spiked with a hint of mint to tingle your taste buds.*

2 cups whole milk

1 teaspoon dried thyme

1 teaspoon dried basil

⅛ teaspoon salt

4 large egg yolks

⅓ cup honey

2 cups whipping cream

1 teaspoon vanilla

½ teaspoon peppermint extract

Combine the milk, thyme, basil, and salt in a medium, heavy saucepan. Scald the milk mixture over medium-high heat, stirring often, for 5 minutes. Remove the pan from the heat and let steep for 1 hour.

Strain the milk mixture through a fine-mesh sieve. Return the milk to a clean, medium, heavy saucepan. Scald the milk once again over medium-high heat, stirring often, for 5 minutes.

While the milk is scalding, whisk together the egg yolks in a medium mixing bowl. Add the honey and whisk until the eggs are light and fluffy. Whisking constantly, add a small amount of the hot milk to the egg mixture. Gradually whisk in the remaining hot milk.

Return the custard mixture to the pan and cook over medium-low heat, stirring often, until the custard is thick enough to coat the back of a spoon, about 8 minutes. Remove the pan from the heat and place in a bowl of ice water to quickly cool the custard. Let the custard cool, stirring often, for 5 minutes.

While the custard is cooling, combine the cream, vanilla, and peppermint in a medium bowl. Stir in the custard mixture. Cover with plastic wrap and press the wrap directly onto the surface of the custard. Refrigerate until completely chilled, at least 4 hours or overnight. The custard may be stored in the refrigerator for up to 3 days.

Freeze the chilled custard mixture in an ice-cream maker according to the manufacturer's instructions. Transfer the ice cream to an airtight container and freeze in the freezer for 2 to 4 hours before serving.

basil ice cream

MAKES ABOUT 1½ QUARTS *Basil is a versatile herb, and relatively easy to grow. In this appealing ice cream, the flavors of fresh and dried basil bring out the best in each other. This ice cream is especially good after a summer barbecue of spicy meats. It's also delicious topped with fresh berries.*

2 cups whole milk

½ cup plus ½ cup sugar

½ cup packed fresh basil leaves

2 teaspoons dried basil

⅛ teaspoon salt

4 large egg yolks

2 cups whipping cream

1 teaspoon vanilla

Combine the milk, ½ cup of the sugar, the fresh basil, dried basil, and salt in a medium, heavy saucepan. Scald the milk mixture over medium-high heat, stirring often, for 5 minutes. Remove the pan from the heat and let steep for 1 hour.

Strain the milk mixture through a fine-mesh sieve. Return the milk to a clean, medium, heavy saucepan. Scald the milk once again over medium-high heat, stirring often, for 5 minutes.

While the milk is scalding, whisk together the egg yolks in a medium mixing bowl. Add the remaining ½ cup of sugar and whisk until the eggs are light and fluffy. Whisking constantly, add a small amount of the hot milk to the egg mixture. Gradually whisk in the remaining hot milk.

Return the custard mixture to the pan and cook over medium-low heat, stirring often, until the custard is thick enough to coat the back of a spoon, about 5 minutes. Remove the pan from the heat and place in a bowl of ice water to quickly cool the custard. Let the custard cool, stirring often, for 5 minutes.

While the custard is cooling, combine the cream and the vanilla in a medium bowl. Stir in the custard mixture. Cover with plastic wrap and press the wrap directly onto the surface of the custard. Refrigerate until completely chilled, at least 4 hours or overnight. The custard may be stored in the refrigerator for up to 3 days.

Freeze the chilled custard mixture in an ice-cream maker according to the manufacturer's instructions. Transfer the ice cream to an airtight container and freeze in the freezer for 2 to 4 hours before serving.

chile-lemongrass ice cream

MAKES ABOUT 1½ QUARTS *Lemongrass may be new to your kitchen, but its unique flavor pairs beautifully with chile pepper. Together, these flavors give this ice cream just enough exotic flair to pique your interest without overpowering your palate. This ice cream is especially good after an Asian-inspired meal.*

4 lemongrass stalks, tough outer leaves removed

2 cups whole milk

½ cup plus ½ cup sugar

1 teaspoon ground mild chile pepper

⅛ teaspoon salt

4 large egg yolks

2 cups whipping cream

1 teaspoon vanilla

Cut the lemongrass into ½-inch pieces, place the pieces in a food processor, and pulse until finely chopped. Combine the lemongrass, milk, ½ cup of the sugar, the chile pepper, and the salt in a medium, heavy saucepan. Scald the milk mixture over medium-high heat, stirring often, for 5 minutes. Remove the pan from the heat and let steep for 1 hour.

Strain the milk mixture through a fine-mesh sieve. Return the milk to a clean, medium, heavy saucepan. Scald the milk once again over medium-high heat, stirring often, for 5 minutes.

While the milk is scalding, whisk together the egg yolks in a medium mixing bowl. Add the remaining ½ cup of sugar and whisk until the eggs are light and fluffy. Whisking constantly, add a small amount of the hot milk to the egg mixture. Gradually whisk in the remaining hot milk.

Return the custard mixture to the pan and cook over medium-low heat, stirring often, until the custard is thick enough to coat the back of a spoon, about 5 minutes. Remove the pan from the heat and place in a bowl of ice water to quickly cool the custard. Let the custard cool, stirring often, for 5 minutes.

While the custard is cooling, combine the cream and the vanilla in a medium bowl. Stir in the custard mixture. Cover with plastic wrap and press the wrap directly onto the surface of the custard. Refrigerate until completely chilled, at least 4 hours or overnight. The custard may be stored in the refrigerator for up to 3 days.

Freeze the chilled custard mixture in an ice-cream maker according to the manufacturer's instructions. Transfer the ice cream to an airtight container and freeze in the freezer for 2 to 4 hours before serving.

pecan spice ice cream

MAKES ABOUT 1¾ QUARTS *If you're fond of butter pecan ice cream, you'll probably love this spiced variation. Clove Candied Pecans give this ice cream a cool new twist.*

2 cups whole milk

½ cup plus ½ cup sugar

1 teaspoon dried lemon zest

⅛ teaspoon salt

4 large egg yolks

2 cups whipping cream

1 teaspoon vanilla

1½ cups Clove Candied Pecans (page 73), chopped

Combine the milk, ½ cup of the sugar, the lemon zest, and the salt in a medium, heavy saucepan. Scald the milk mixture over medium-high heat, stirring often, for 5 minutes.

While the milk is scalding, whisk together the egg yolks in a medium mixing bowl. Add the remaining ½ cup of sugar and whisk until the eggs are light and fluffy. Whisking constantly, add a small amount of the hot milk to the egg mixture. Gradually whisk in the remaining hot milk.

Return the custard mixture to the pan and cook over medium-low heat, stirring often, until the custard is thick enough to coat the back of a spoon, about 5 minutes. Remove the pan from the heat and place in a bowl of ice water to quickly cool the custard. Let the custard cool, stirring often, for 5 minutes.

While the custard is cooling, combine the cream and the vanilla in a medium bowl. Stir in the custard mixture. Cover with plastic wrap and press the wrap directly onto the surface of the custard. Refrigerate until completely chilled, at least 4 hours or overnight. The custard may be stored in the refrigerator for up to 3 days.

Freeze the chilled custard mixture in an ice-cream maker according to the manufacturer's instructions. Stir the pecans into the soft, creamy ice cream during the last minute of mixing; churn until just mixed. Transfer the ice cream to an airtight container and freeze in the freezer for 2 to 4 hours before serving.

spiced apple ice cream

MAKES ABOUT 1 QUART *This frozen treat combines the appeal of an apple pie and the satisfaction of a smooth ice cream. It's delicious by itself, and it's awesome in Caramel Apple Sundaes (page 54).*

ice cream:

1 cup whole milk

¼ cup plus ¼ cup sugar

½ teaspoon dried lemon zest

Pinch of salt

2 large egg yolks

1 cup whipping cream

½ teaspoon vanilla

spiced apples:

2 large Granny Smith apples, peeled, cored, thinly sliced, and cut into quarters (about 2 cups)

⅓ cup sugar

1 teaspoon vanilla

1 teaspoon ground cinnamon

1 teaspoon ground allspice

½ teaspoon dried lemon zest

⅛ teaspoon salt

To make the ice cream, combine the milk, ¼ cup of the sugar, the lemon zest, and the salt in a medium, heavy saucepan. Scald the milk mixture over medium-high heat, stirring often, for 5 minutes.

While the milk is scalding, whisk together the egg yolks in a medium mixing bowl. Add the remaining ¼ cup of sugar and whisk until the eggs are light and fluffy. Whisking constantly, add a small amount of the hot milk to the egg mixture. Gradually whisk in the remaining hot milk.

Return the custard mixture to the pan and cook over medium-low heat, stirring often, until the custard is thick enough to coat the back of a spoon, about 5 minutes. Remove the pan from the heat and place in a bowl of ice water to quickly cool the custard. Let the custard cool, stirring often, for 5 minutes.

While the custard is cooling, combine the cream and the vanilla in a medium bowl. Stir in the custard mixture. Cover with plastic wrap and press the wrap directly onto the surface of the custard. Refrigerate until completely chilled, at least 4 hours or overnight. The custard may be stored in the refrigerator for up to 3 days.

(continued on page 14)

(continued)

To make the spiced apples, combine the apples, sugar, vanilla, cinnamon, allspice, lemon zest, and salt in a medium, heavy saucepan. Cook the apples over medium heat, stirring often, until the apples are tender and all the liquid is gone, about 10 minutes. Let the apples cool and then place them in the refrigerator to chill.

Freeze the chilled custard mixture in an ice-cream maker according to the manufacturer's instructions. Add the spiced apples to the soft, creamy ice cream during the last minute of mixing; churn until just mixed. Transfer the ice cream to an airtight container and freeze in the freezer for 2 to 4 hours before serving.

brown sugar–ginger ice cream

MAKES ABOUT 1½ QUARTS *Brown sugar gives this ice cream a hint of molasses, while the ginger lends just the right tingle to the mix. All in all, we find this to be an irresistible combination. It's good all on its own, it's delicious with pound cake and peaches, and it's sensational in Chocolate–Ginger Cookie Ice-Cream Sandwiches (page 45).*

2 cups whole milk

½ cup plus ½ cup firmly packed brown sugar (light or dark)

1 teaspoon ground ginger

⅛ teaspoon salt

4 large egg yolks

2 cups whipping cream

1 teaspoon vanilla

Combine the milk, ½ cup of the brown sugar, the ginger, and the salt in a medium, heavy saucepan. Scald the milk mixture over medium-high heat, stirring often, for 5 minutes.

While the milk is scalding, whisk together the egg yolks in a medium mixing bowl. Add the remaining ½ cup of brown sugar and whisk until the eggs are light and fluffy. Whisking constantly, add a small amount of the hot milk to the egg mixture. Gradually whisk in the remaining hot milk.

Return the custard mixture to the pan and cook over medium-low heat, stirring often, until the custard is thick enough to coat the back of a spoon, about 5 minutes. Remove the pan from the heat and place in a bowl of ice water to quickly cool the custard. Let the custard cool, stirring often, for 5 minutes.

While the custard is cooling, combine the cream and the vanilla in a medium bowl. Stir in the custard mixture. Cover with plastic wrap and press the wrap directly onto the surface of the custard. Refrigerate until completely chilled, at least 4 hours or overnight. The custard may be stored in the refrigerator for up to 3 days.

Freeze the chilled custard mixture in an ice-cream maker according to the manufacturer's instructions. Transfer the ice cream to an airtight container and freeze in the freezer for 2 to 4 hours before serving.

brown sugar and spiced banana ice cream

MAKES ABOUT 1½ QUARTS *Sweet but mellow, bananas play well with spices. Together, they turn plain vanilla into a spice-enlightened taste adventure. You'll find many reasons to make this spiced cream, a delightful variation on that beloved classic, Bananas Foster.*

1 medium ripe banana

¼ cup plus 1¾ cups whole milk

½ cup plus ½ cup firmly packed brown sugar (light or dark)

1 teaspoon ground cinnamon

1 teaspoon ground cardamom

1 teaspoon ground nutmeg

⅛ teaspoon salt

4 large egg yolks

2 cups whipping cream

1 teaspoon vanilla

Puree the banana and ¼ cup of the milk in a food processor until smooth. Combine the banana puree, the remaining 1¾ cups of milk, ½ cup of the brown sugar, the cinnamon, cardamom, nutmeg, and salt in a medium, heavy saucepan. Scald the milk mixture over medium-high heat, stirring often, for 5 minutes.

While the milk is scalding, whisk together the egg yolks in a medium mixing bowl. Add the remaining ½ cup of brown sugar and whisk until the eggs are light and fluffy. Whisking constantly, add a small amount of the hot milk to the egg mixture. Gradually whisk in the remaining hot milk.

Return the custard mixture to the pan and cook over medium-low heat, stirring often, until the custard is thick enough to coat the back of a spoon, about 5 minutes. Remove the pan from the heat and place in a bowl of ice water to quickly cool the custard. Let the custard cool, stirring often, for 5 minutes.

While the custard is cooling, combine the cream and the vanilla in a medium bowl. Stir in the custard mixture. Cover with plastic wrap and press the wrap directly onto the surface of the custard. Refrigerate until completely chilled, at least 4 hours or overnight. The custard may be stored in the refrigerator for up to 3 days.

Freeze the chilled custard mixture in an ice-cream maker according to the manufacturer's instructions. Transfer the ice cream to an airtight container and freeze in the freezer for 2 to 4 hours before serving.

almond ice cream with turmeric, cardamom, and cloves

MAKES ABOUT 1½ QUARTS *This may seem like an exotic ice cream, but we have found that even unadventurous eaters will ask for more. The first thing you'll notice about this enticingly spiced ice cream is its bright yellow-orange color. Welcome to the joys of turmeric, a spice that rarely gets star billing but can really shine when given the opportunity. Turmeric is probably best known for lending color to mustard, but it's an essential part of many spice blends, especially curries. In this ice cream, it provides a hint of earthy intrigue that works beautifully with the cardamom and cloves.*

2 cups whole milk

½ cup plus ½ cup sugar

1 teaspoon ground turmeric

1 teaspoon ground cardamom

½ teaspoon ground cloves

⅛ teaspoon salt

4 large egg yolks

2 cups whipping cream

1 teaspoon almond extract

½ cup slivered almonds, toasted (see Note)

Combine the milk, ½ cup of the sugar, the turmeric, cardamom, cloves, and salt in a medium, heavy saucepan. Scald the milk mixture over medium-high heat, stirring often, for 5 minutes. While the milk is scalding, whisk together the egg yolks in a medium mixing bowl. Add the remaining ½ cup of sugar and whisk until the eggs are light and fluffy.

Whisking constantly, add a small amount of the hot milk to the egg mixture. Gradually whisk in the remaining hot milk. Return the custard mixture to the pan and cook over medium-low heat, stirring often, until the custard is thick enough to coat the back of a spoon, about 5 minutes. Remove the pan from the heat and place in a bowl of ice water to quickly cool the custard. Let the custard cool, stirring often, for 5 minutes.

While the custard is cooling, combine the cream and almond extract in a medium bowl. Stir in the custard mixture. Cover with plastic wrap and press the wrap directly onto the surface of the custard. Refrigerate until completely chilled, at least 4 hours or overnight. The custard may be stored in the refrigerator for up to 3 days.

Freeze the chilled custard mixture in an ice-cream maker according to the manufacturer's instructions. Transfer the ice cream to an airtight container and freeze in the freezer for 2 to 4 hours before serving.

Note: To toast sliced almonds, place a rack in the middle of the oven and preheat the oven to 350°F. Spread the sliced almonds evenly on a baking sheet and toast for about 5 minutes, or until the almonds just begin to turn golden brown and fragrant. There is a fine line between toasting nuts and burning them, so watch them carefully.

spiced chocolate chip cookie dough ice cream

MAKES ABOUT 1¾ QUARTS *We like cookie dough ice cream, but we have to admit that the addition of a few strategic spices elevates this treat to the level of a major addiction.*

ice cream:

2 cups whole milk

½ cup plus ½ cup sugar

1 teaspoon dried lemon zest

⅛ teaspoon salt

4 large egg yolks

2 cups whipping cream

1 teaspoon vanilla

cookie dough:

4 tablespoons (½ stick) unsalted butter, at room temperature

⅓ cup firmly packed brown sugar (light or dark)

⅓ cup granulated sugar

2 tablespoons milk

1 teaspoon vanilla

1 teaspoon ground cinnamon

1 teaspoon ground cloves

¼ teaspoon salt

1 cup all-purpose flour

½ cup semisweet mini chocolate chips

To make the ice cream, combine the milk, ½ cup of the sugar, the lemon zest, and the salt in a medium, heavy saucepan. Scald the milk mixture over medium-high heat, stirring often, for 5 minutes.

While the milk is scalding, whisk together the egg yolks in a medium mixing bowl. Add the remaining ½ cup of sugar and whisk until the eggs are light and fluffy. Whisking constantly, add a small amount of the hot milk to the egg mixture. Gradually whisk in the remaining hot milk.

Return the custard mixture to the pan and cook over medium-low heat, stirring often, until the custard is thick enough to coat the back of a spoon, about 5 minutes. Remove the pan from the heat and place in a bowl of ice water to quickly cool the custard. Let the custard cool, stirring often, for 5 minutes.

While the custard is cooling, combine the cream and the vanilla in a medium bowl. Stir in the custard mixture. Cover with plastic wrap and press the wrap directly onto the surface of the custard. Refrigerate until completely chilled, at least 4 hours or overnight. The custard may be stored in the refrigerator for up to 3 days.

To make the cookie dough, cream the butter and sugar in a large mixing bowl until light and fluffy. Add the milk, vanilla, cinnamon, cloves, and salt to the butter mixture and beat together. Gradually beat in the flour until combined. Stir in the chocolate chips. Form small bits (¼ to ⅛ teaspoonfuls) of the cookie dough into balls and freeze for 1 hour, or until firm. (Note: Larger dough balls will produce larger bursts of spice in the finished cream.)

Freeze the chilled custard mixture in an ice-cream maker according to the manufacturer's instructions. Gently fold the frozen cookie dough into the soft, creamy ice cream. Transfer the ice cream to an airtight container and freeze in the freezer for 2 to 4 hours before serving.

cinnamon-raspberry cheesecake ice cream

MAKES ABOUT 1 QUART *Raspberries, lemon zest, and cinnamon combine to make this cheesecake ice cream irresistible. We love the cinnamon-raspberry combination, but feel free to use another spice (maybe allspice or cardamom) and another berry instead.*

1 cup whole milk

¼ cup plus ¼ cup sugar

½ teaspoon plus 1½ teaspoons dried lemon zest

Pinch of salt

2 large egg yolks

1 cup whipping cream

½ teaspoon vanilla

12 ounces cream cheese, at room temperature

1 tablespoon freshly squeezed lemon juice

1 teaspoon ground cinnamon

1 cup raspberries

Combine the milk, ¼ cup of the sugar, ½ teaspoon of the lemon zest, and the salt in a medium, heavy saucepan. Scald the milk mixture over medium-high heat, stirring often, for 5 minutes.

While the milk is scalding, whisk together the egg yolks in a medium mixing bowl. Add the remaining ¼ cup of sugar and whisk until the eggs are light and fluffy. Whisking constantly, add a small amount of the hot milk to the egg mixture. Gradually whisk in the remaining hot milk.

Return the custard mixture to the pan and cook over medium-low heat, stirring often, until the custard is thick enough to coat the back of a spoon, about 5 minutes. Remove the pan from the heat and place in a bowl of ice water to quickly cool the custard. Let the custard cool, stirring often, for 5 minutes.

While the custard is cooling, combine the cream and the vanilla in a medium bowl. Stir in the custard mixture. Cover with plastic wrap and press the wrap directly onto the surface of the custard. Refrigerate until completely chilled, at least 4 hours or overnight. The custard may be stored in the refrigerator for up to 3 days.

Once the custard is completely chilled, beat together the cream cheese, lemon juice, the remaining 1½ teaspoons of lemon zest, and cinnamon in a large mixing bowl until smooth and creamy. Gradually beat in the chilled custard mixture.

Freeze the mixture in an ice-cream maker according to the manufacturer's instructions. Gently fold the raspberries into the soft, creamy ice cream. Transfer the ice cream to an airtight container and freeze in the freezer for 2 to 4 hours before serving.

white chocolate–allspice ice cream

MAKES ABOUT 1½ QUARTS *If you have any remaining doubts about spicing up ice cream, this amazing combination of flavors will persuade you that spices and ice cream can bring out the best in each other. Allspice carries hints of cinnamon, cloves, and nutmeg, but this Caribbean berry has an enchantment all its own. It's the perfect partner for white chocolate, and together these soul mates create an ice cream that you'll want to make over and over again.*

2 cups whole milk

¼ cup plus ½ cup sugar

2 teaspoons ground allspice

⅛ teaspoon salt

4 large egg yolks

4 ounces white chocolate, finely chopped

2 cups whipping cream

1 teaspoon vanilla

Combine the milk, ¼ cup of the sugar, the allspice, and the salt in a medium, heavy saucepan. Scald the milk mixture over medium-high heat, stirring often, for 5 minutes.

While the milk is scalding, whisk together the egg yolks in a medium mixing bowl. Add the remaining ½ cup of sugar and whisk until the eggs are light and fluffy. Whisking constantly, add a small amount of the hot milk to the egg mixture. Gradually whisk in the remaining hot milk.

Return the custard mixture to the pan and cook over medium-low heat, stirring often, until the custard is thick enough to coat the back of a spoon, about 5 minutes. Remove the pan from the heat and add the chocolate. Whisk until the chocolate melts and the custard is smooth. Place the pan in a bowl of ice water to quickly cool the custard. Let the custard cool, stirring often, for 5 minutes.

While the custard is cooling, combine the cream and the vanilla in a medium bowl. Stir in the custard mixture. Cover with plastic wrap and press the wrap directly onto the surface of the custard. Refrigerate until completely chilled, at least 4 hours or overnight. The custard may be stored in the refrigerator for up to 3 days.

Freeze the chilled custard mixture in an ice-cream maker according to the manufacturer's instructions. Transfer the ice cream to an airtight container and freeze in the freezer for 2 to 4 hours before serving.

dark chocolate–anise ice cream

MAKES ABOUT 1½ QUARTS *Chocolate and cocoa powder combine to make this ice cream especially rich and chocolaty. Accent it with anise seed for added allure. This is a great base for chocolate ice cream, and it works well with other spices, too. If you like, substitute cardamom, cloves, or another spice for the anise seed.*

2 cups whole milk

½ cup plus ½ cup sugar

2 teaspoons anise seed

⅛ teaspoon salt

4 large egg yolks

⅓ cup unsweetened cocoa powder (preferably Dutch-processed)

3 ounces bittersweet or semisweet chocolate, finely chopped

2 cups whipping cream

1 teaspoon vanilla

Combine the milk, ½ cup of the sugar, the anise seed, and the salt in a medium, heavy saucepan. Scald the milk mixture over medium-high heat, stirring often, for 5 minutes. Remove the pan from the heat and let steep for 1 hour.

Strain the milk mixture through a fine-mesh sieve. Return the milk to a clean medium, heavy saucepan. Scald the milk once again over medium-high heat, stirring often, for 5 minutes.

While the milk is scalding, whisk together the egg yolks in a medium mixing bowl. Add the remaining ½ cup of sugar and the cocoa powder and whisk until the eggs are light and fluffy. Whisking constantly, add a small amount of the hot milk to the egg mixture. Gradually whisk in the remaining hot milk.

Return the custard mixture to the pan and cook over medium-low heat, stirring often, until the custard is thick enough to coat the back of a spoon, about 5 minutes. Remove the pan from the heat and add the chocolate. Whisk until the chocolate melts and the custard is smooth. Place the pan in a bowl of ice water to quickly cool the custard. Let the custard cool, stirring often, for 5 minutes.

While the custard is cooling, combine the cream and the vanilla in a medium bowl. Stir in the custard mixture. Cover with plastic wrap and press the wrap directly onto the surface of the custard. Refrigerate until completely chilled, at least 4 hours or overnight. The custard may be stored in the refrigerator for up to 3 days.

Freeze the chilled custard mixture in an ice-cream maker according to the manufacturer's instructions. Transfer the ice cream to an airtight container and freeze in the freezer for 2 to 4 hours before serving.

chocolate ice cream with cumin and fennel

MAKES ABOUT 1½ QUARTS *Cumin is not likely to be the first flavor that springs to mind when you think of spicing up ice cream. But as an essential spice in some of the world's great cuisines, from India to the Middle East to Latin America, it's surely one of the world's most ubiquitous flavors—so why not give it a spice cream to star in?*

2 cups whole milk

¼ cup plus ½ cup sugar

1 teaspoon ground cumin

1 teaspoon fennel seed

⅛ teaspoon salt

4 large egg yolks

4 ounces semisweet chocolate, finely chopped

2 cups whipping cream

1 teaspoon vanilla

Combine the milk, ¼ cup of the sugar, the cumin, fennel seed, and salt in a medium, heavy saucepan. Scald the milk mixture over medium-high heat, stirring often, for 5 minutes.

While the milk is scalding, whisk together the egg yolks in a medium mixing bowl. Add the remaining ½ cup of sugar and whisk until the eggs are light and fluffy. Whisking constantly, add a small amount of the hot milk to the egg mixture. Gradually whisk in the remaining hot milk.

Return the custard mixture to the pan and cook over medium-low heat, stirring often, until the custard is thick enough to coat the back of a spoon, about 5 minutes. Remove the pan from the heat and add the chocolate. Whisk until the chocolate melts and the custard is smooth. Place the pan in a bowl of ice water to quickly cool the custard. Let the custard cool, stirring often, for 5 minutes.

While the custard is cooling, combine the cream and the vanilla in a medium bowl. Stir in the custard mixture. Cover with plastic wrap and press the wrap directly onto the surface of the custard. Refrigerate until completely chilled, at least 4 hours or overnight. The custard may be stored in the refrigerator for up to 3 days.

Freeze the chilled custard mixture in an ice-cream maker according to the manufacturer's instructions. Transfer the ice cream to an airtight container and freeze in the freezer for 2 to 4 hours before serving.

three-spice chocolate ice cream

MAKES ABOUT 1½ QUARTS *Chocolate is a great background for spices, and this ice cream features a bold but well-blended trio of cloves, cardamom, and cinnamon. They do their work so well you might have trouble loving plain old chocolate again.*

2 cups whole milk

½ cup plus ½ cup sugar

1 teaspoon ground cloves

1 teaspoon ground cardamom

1 teaspoon ground cinnamon

⅛ teaspoon salt

4 large egg yolks

⅓ cup unsweetened cocoa powder

3 ounces bittersweet or semisweet chocolate, finely chopped

2 cups whipping cream

1 teaspoon vanilla

Combine the milk, ½ cup of the sugar, the cloves, cardamom, cinnamon, and salt in a medium, heavy saucepan. Scald the milk mixture over medium-high heat, stirring often, for 5 minutes. Remove the pan from the heat and let steep for 1 hour.

Strain the milk mixture through a fine-mesh sieve. Return the milk to a clean medium, heavy saucepan. Scald the milk once again over medium-high heat, stirring often, for 5 minutes.

While the milk is scalding, whisk together the egg yolks in a medium mixing bowl. Add the remaining ½ cup of sugar and the cocoa powder and whisk until the eggs are light and fluffy. Whisking constantly, add a small amount of the hot milk to the egg mixture. Gradually whisk in the remaining hot milk.

Return the custard mixture to the pan and cook over medium-low heat, stirring often, until the custard is thick enough to coat the back of a spoon, about 5 minutes. Remove the pan from the heat and add the chocolate. Whisk until the chocolate melts and the custard is smooth. Place the pan in a bowl of ice water to quickly cool the custard. Let the custard cool, stirring often, for 5 minutes.

While the custard is cooling, combine the cream and the vanilla in a medium bowl. Stir in the custard mixture. Cover with plastic wrap and press the wrap directly onto the surface of the custard. Refrigerate until completely chilled, at least 4 hours or overnight. The custard may be stored in the refrigerator for up to 3 days.

Freeze the chilled custard mixture in an ice-cream maker according to the manufacturer's instructions. Transfer the ice cream to an airtight container and freeze in the freezer for 2 to 4 hours before serving.

| sorbets and frozen yogurts |

Can you take the cream out of ice cream and still have something good? We say yes! This chapter features several recipes based on coconut milk, as well as some traditional sorbets. They will appeal to most anyone who loves a frozen treat, but they're perfect if you're a vegan, lactose intolerant, or just need a nondairy delight.

We're also including a couple of frozen yogurts, which we've come to depend on for two big reasons—they're delicious and they're easy. What more can you ask than that?

chocolate–chocolate chip–coconut sorbet

MAKES ABOUT 1 QUART *Our friend Amy inspired us to experiment with chocolate coconut sorbet. These sorbets offer a delicious change of pace from ice creams based on milk and eggs. They are also simpler to make, since there's no need to heat the custard and cook the eggs. This chocolate-coconut sorbet is especially delicious—and a good reason to make coconut milk a staple in your pantry. It's also proof that nondairy treats can be wickedly good.*

¾ cup sugar

¾ cup water

⅛ teaspoon salt

1 teaspoon ground cinnamon

½ teaspoon ground cloves (optional)

¾ cup plus ¼ cup mini semisweet chocolate chips

1 (14-ounce) can coconut milk

¼ cup sweetened flaked coconut

¼ teaspoon vanilla

Combine the sugar, water, and salt in a medium, heavy saucepan. Heat the mixture over medium heat, stirring gently, until the sugar has completely dissolved and the syrup is clear, about 5 minutes. Whisk in the cinnamon and the cloves if using, and continue to cook, whisking continually, for 1 minute.

Remove the pan from the heat and add ¾ cup of the chocolate chips. Whisk until the chocolate melts and the mixture is smooth. Place the pan in a bowl of ice water to quickly cool the mixture. Let it cool, stirring often, for 5 minutes.

Combine the coconut milk, flaked coconut, and vanilla in a medium bowl. Add the chocolate mixture and whisk until the chocolate and coconut milk are completely mixed. Cover and refrigerate until completely chilled, at least 4 hours or overnight. The sorbet mixture may be stored in the refrigerator for up to 3 days.

Freeze the chilled sorbet mixture in an ice-cream maker according to the manufacturer's instructions. Add the remaining ¼ cup of chocolate chips during the last 5 minutes of mixing in the ice-cream maker. Transfer the sorbet to an airtight container and freeze in the freezer for 2 to 4 hours before serving.

coconut-ginger sorbet

MAKES ABOUT 3 CUPS *Ginger and coconut bring out the best in each other, as you will see in this delightful sorbet. If you like, kick up the flavor with Ancho-Lime Syrup (page 70), or complement the flavor with Cinnamon Syrup (page 69).*

¾ cup sugar

¾ cup water

1 teaspoon ground ginger

⅛ teaspoon salt

1 (14-ounce) can coconut milk

¼ cup sweetened flaked coconut

¼ teaspoon vanilla

Combine the sugar, water, ginger, and salt in a medium, heavy saucepan. Heat the sugar mixture over medium heat, stirring gently, until the sugar has completely dissolved and the syrup is clear, about 5 minutes. Remove the pan from the heat and let steep for 1 hour.

Combine the coconut milk, flaked coconut, and vanilla in a medium bowl. Strain the syrup mixture through a fine-mesh sieve into the coconut milk mixture. Whisk until the syrup and coconut milk are completely mixed. Cover and refrigerate until completely chilled, at least 4 hours or overnight. The sorbet mixture may be stored in the refrigerator for up to 3 days.

Freeze the chilled sorbet mixture in an ice-cream maker according to the manufacturer's instructions. Transfer the sorbet to an airtight container and freeze in the freezer for 2 to 4 hours before serving.

marjoram-mint-coconut sorbet

MAKES ABOUT 3 CUPS *Marjoram is gentler and less assertive than its more familiar cousin, oregano. Mint brings out its sweetest side, yielding a sorbet that is both surprising and satisfying. For a refreshing Coconut–Mint Chip Sorbet, add ¼ cup of mini semisweet chocolate chips during the last 5 minutes of mixing in the ice-cream maker.*

¾ cup sugar

¾ cup water

1 teaspoon dried marjoram

⅛ teaspoon salt

1 (14-ounce) can coconut milk

¼ cup sweetened flaked coconut

¼ teaspoon peppermint extract

¼ teaspoon vanilla

Combine the sugar, water, marjoram, and salt in a medium, heavy saucepan. Heat the sugar mixture over medium heat, stirring gently, until the sugar has completely dissolved and the syrup is clear, about 5 minutes. Remove the pan from the heat and let steep for 1 hour.

Combine the coconut milk, flaked coconut, peppermint, and vanilla in a medium bowl. Strain the syrup mixture through a fine-mesh sieve into the coconut milk mixture. Whisk until the syrup and coconut milk are completely mixed. Cover and refrigerate until completely chilled, at least 4 hours or overnight. The sorbet mixture may be stored in the refrigerator for up to 3 days.

Freeze the chilled sorbet mixture in an ice-cream maker according to the manufacturer's instructions. Transfer the sorbet to an airtight container and freeze in the freezer for 2 to 4 hours before serving.

pineapple-coconut sorbet

MAKES ABOUT 1½ QUARTS *Fresh pineapple is the star of this wickedly good sorbet, but it's the ginger, lemon, and zest that really make it shine.*

1 cup sugar

¼ cup water

⅛ teaspoon salt

1 (3-pound) pineapple, peeled, cored, and cubed

3 tablespoons freshly squeezed lemon juice

1 (14-ounce) can coconut milk

¼ cup sweetened flaked coconut

1 teaspoon ground ginger

1 teaspoon dried lemon zest

¼ teaspoon vanilla

Combine the sugar, water, and salt in a medium, heavy saucepan. Heat the mixture over medium heat, stirring gently, until the sugar has completely dissolved and the syrup is clear, about 5 minutes. Remove the pan from the heat and place in a bowl of ice water to quickly cool the syrup. Let it cool, stirring often, for 5 minutes.

While the syrup is cooling, place the pineapple and the lemon juice in a food processor and puree until smooth. Strain the pineapple puree through a mesh sieve into a large bowl. Add the syrup, coconut milk, flaked coconut, ginger, lemon zest, and vanilla to the puree and whisk until fully mixed. Cover and refrigerate until completely chilled, at least 4 hours or overnight. The sorbet mixture may be stored in the refrigerator for 1 day.

Freeze the chilled sorbet mixture in an ice-cream maker according to the manufacturer's instructions. Transfer the sorbet to an airtight container and freeze in the freezer for 2 to 4 hours before serving.

mango sorbet with cumin and cinnamon

MAKES ABOUT 3 CUPS *This recipe for mango sorbet is a winner even without the spices. But cinnamon and cumin lend an appealingly adventurous streak to mangoes, so it's a shame not to let the spices shine. We like the full teaspoon of each spice, but it's fine to start with ½ teaspoon.*

1 cup sugar

1 cup water

⅛ teaspoon salt

½ to 1 teaspoon ground cumin

½ to 1 teaspoon ground cinnamon

3 mangoes, peeled, pitted, and cubed

2 tablespoons freshly squeezed lemon juice

Combine the sugar, water, and salt in a medium, heavy saucepan. Heat the mixture over medium heat, stirring gently, until the sugar has completely dissolved and the syrup is clear, about 5 minutes.

Whisk in the cumin and cinnamon, and continue to cook, whisking continually, for 1 minute. Remove the pan from the heat and place in a bowl of ice water to quickly cool the syrup. Let it cool, stirring often, for 5 minutes.

While the syrup is cooling, place the mangoes and the lemon juice in a food processor and puree until smooth. Strain the mango puree through a mesh sieve into a medium bowl. Add the syrup to the puree and whisk until smooth. Cover and refrigerate until completely chilled, at least 4 hours or overnight. The sorbet mixture may be stored in the refrigerator for 1 day.

Freeze the chilled sorbet mixture in an ice-cream maker according to the manufacturer's instructions. Transfer the sorbet to an airtight container and freeze in the freezer for 2 to 4 hours before serving.

chile-orange-chocolate sorbet

. . . .

MAKES ABOUT 2½ CUPS *The double dose of flavor from cocoa powder and chocolate gives this sorbet such a creamy texture that it's hard to tell there's no cream. Any chocolate lover will be glad to have this recipe, but if you're dairy-averse, you've just found a treasure.*

2 cups water

¾ cup sugar

⅔ cup unsweetened cocoa powder

3 teaspoons dried orange zest

½ to 1 teaspoon ground mild chile pepper

⅛ teaspoon salt

4 ounces semisweet chocolate, finely chopped

1 teaspoon vanilla

Combine the water, sugar, cocoa powder, orange zest, chile pepper, and salt in a large, heavy saucepan. Heat the mixture over medium heat, whisking frequently, until the sugar has completely dissolved and the mixture comes to a boil, about 5 minutes. Remove the pan from the heat and add the chocolate and the vanilla.

Whisk until the chocolate melts and the sorbet mixture is smooth. Place the pan in a bowl of ice water to quickly cool the mixture. Let it cool, stirring often, for 5 minutes. Cover and refrigerate until completely chilled, at least 6 hours or overnight. The sorbet mixture may be stored in the refrigerator for up to 3 days.

Freeze the chilled sorbet mixture in an ice-cream maker according to the manufacturer's instructions. Transfer the sorbet to an airtight container and freeze in the freezer for 2 to 4 hours before serving.

strawberry-cinnamon frozen yogurt

MAKES ABOUT 1 QUART *Frozen yogurt can be as easy as it is delicious. The tangy sweetness of this frozen treat perfectly complements the combination of strawberries and cinnamon, a pairing that is universally admired.*

3 cups Greek-style yogurt
(see Note)

1½ cups sugar

¼ cup freshly squeezed
lemon juice

1 teaspoon vanilla

1 teaspoon ground
cinnamon

1 teaspoon dried lemon zest

⅛ teaspoon salt

1 cup fresh strawberries,
quartered and thinly sliced

Combine the yogurt, sugar, lemon juice, vanilla, cinnamon, lemon zest, and salt in a medium bowl and whisk until smooth. Freeze the mixture in an ice-cream maker according to the manufacturer's instructions. Add the strawberries during the last minute of mixing in the ice-cream maker. Transfer the yogurt to an airtight container and freeze in the freezer for 2 to 4 hours before serving.

Note: Greek-style yogurt has become much more readily available in recent years. However, if you are unable to find it in your local markets, you can make your own.

To make 3 cups of Greek-style yogurt, line a mesh strainer with a few layers of cheesecloth and set it into a large bowl. Place 6 cups of plain whole-milk yogurt into the cheesecloth. Gather the ends of the cheesecloth and fold them over the yogurt. Refrigerate the yogurt for at least 6 hours or overnight. Scoop the strained yogurt from the cheesecloth and use it immediately or store it in an airtight container in the refrigerator for up to one week.

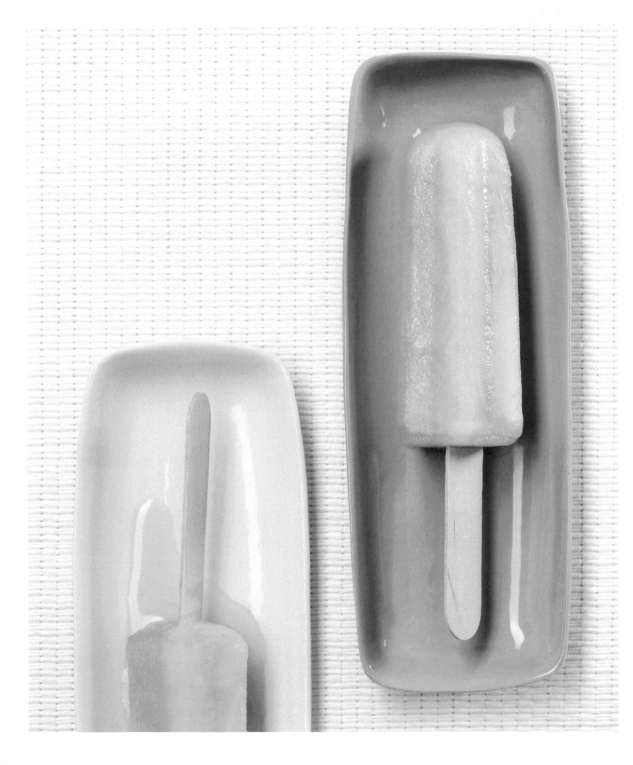

pink grapefruit–tarragon sorbet

MAKES ABOUT 1 QUART *This is an exceptionally refreshing and versatile sorbet and a terrific combination of flavors. It's a perfect palate cleanser, but it works nicely as a dessert as well.*

1 cup sugar

1 cup water

1 to 2 teaspoons dried tarragon

⅛ teaspoon salt

1¾ cups freshly squeezed pink or ruby red grapefruit juice

Combine the sugar, water, tarragon, and salt in a medium, heavy saucepan. Heat the mixture over medium heat, stirring gently, until the sugar has completely dissolved and the syrup is clear, about 5 minutes. Remove the pan from the heat and let the syrup steep for 1 hour.

Strain the syrup through a mesh sieve into a medium bowl. Add the grapefruit juice to the syrup and whisk until completely mixed. Cover and refrigerate until completely chilled, at least 4 hours or overnight. The sorbet mixture may be stored in the refrigerator for 1 day.

Freeze the chilled sorbet mixture in an ice-cream maker according to the manufacturer's instructions. Transfer the sorbet to an airtight container and freeze in the freezer for 2 to 4 hours before serving.

Note: This sorbet also makes a delightful popsicle. Rather than freezing the sorbet mixture in an ice-cream maker, pour it into popsicle molds and freeze in the freezer.

lemon-allspice frozen yogurt

MAKES ABOUT 1 QUART *Allspice and lemon zest pair nicely with yogurt's tart appeal. Serve this frozen treat with Cardamom Snickerdoodles (page 50) and fresh fruit for an elegant and healthy dessert.*

3 cups Greek-style yogurt (see Note on page 39)

1½ cups sugar

¼ cup freshly squeezed lemon juice

1 teaspoon vanilla

1 teaspoon ground allspice

1 teaspoon dried lemon zest

⅛ teaspoon salt

Combine the yogurt, sugar, lemon juice, vanilla, allspice, lemon zest, and salt in a medium bowl and whisk until smooth. Freeze the yogurt mixture in an ice-cream maker according to the manufacturer's instructions. Transfer the yogurt to an airtight container and freeze in the freezer for 2 to 4 hours before serving.

Ice cream is such a wonder in itself that a contrarian might be indulged for wondering why people don't just enjoy it as is. But even contrarians wouldn't really want to live without banana splits, or sinfully delicious sundaes, or even floats and milkshakes.

The wonder of ice cream is just that—the little voice it inspires inside us that says, "I wonder how this would taste with ice cream?"

We'll go you one or two or even three steps better in this chapter. How about spice-cream sundaes or floats, or a curried banana split, or a fabulous frozen spice-cream cheesecake?

If spices take ice cream to a new level, these variations on old favorites will take spice cream to new altitudes of delight.

chocolate-ginger cookies

MAKES ABOUT 1 DOZEN COOKIES *We think spices and chocolate are an irresistible combination, and we especially like the ginger in these cookies. The double dose gives them an appealing tingle—perfect for ice-cream sandwiches. However, feel free to cut back the ginger to 1 teaspoon and let it blend in with the cinnamon and cloves. Either way, we think you'll call these cookies a winner.*

6 tablespoons unsalted butter, at room temperature

½ cup sugar

2 tablespoons milk

1 tablespoon vanilla

1 cup all-purpose flour

⅓ cup unsweetened cocoa powder

2 teaspoons ground ginger

1 teaspoon ground cinnamon

1 teaspoon ground cloves

¼ teaspoon baking powder

¼ teaspoon salt

Preheat the oven to 350°F. Cream the butter and sugar in a large mixing bowl until light and fluffy. Add the milk and the vanilla and beat until combined. Sift the flour, cocoa powder, ginger, cinnamon, cloves, baking powder, and salt into a medium bowl. Gradually add the flour mixture to the butter mixture and beat until the dough is combined.

Scoop the dough by rounded tablespoons and roll into generous 1-inch balls. Place the dough balls 2 inches apart on an ungreased baking sheet. Use the bottom of a glass to flatten the dough balls into 2½-inch round circles, placing a small piece of waxed paper between the glass and the dough to prevent sticking, if necessary. The finished cookies will need to be completely flat like an ice-cream sandwich wafer. Bake the cookies for 12 minutes, or until the cookies spring back when lightly touched. Remove the cookies from the oven and allow them to cool for 5 minutes before removing them from the baking sheet. Cool completely before making the ice-cream sandwiches.

chocolate–ginger cookie ice-cream sandwiches

MAKES 6 SANDWICHES *These chocolate-ginger cookies are good with almost any ice cream. But you've got to start somewhere, and we think you'll agree these cookies and Brown Sugar– Ginger Ice Cream make a sensational pair.*

12 Chocolate-Ginger Cookies (page 44)

2 to 3 cups Brown Sugar– Ginger Ice Cream (page 15) or your favorite spice cream, slightly softened

Place one cookie top side down. Scoop ⅓ to ½ cup of ice cream onto the cookie. Place another cookie top side up on the ice cream and press gently to flatten the ice cream between the two cookies. Serve the ice-cream sandwiches immediately.

oatmeal-raisin cookies

MAKES 2 DOZEN COOKIES *We love a good oatmeal cookie, especially when it's enhanced by two of our favorite spices, cinnamon and cloves. This cookie is delicious with spice cream, and it makes a righteously good ice-cream sandwich (page 47).*

8 tablespoons (1 stick) unsalted butter, at room temperature

½ cup firmly packed brown sugar (light or dark)

½ cup granulated sugar

1 egg

2 teaspoons vanilla

1 cup all-purpose flour

1 teaspoon ground cinnamon

1 teaspoon ground cloves

½ teaspoon salt

½ teaspoon baking powder

½ teaspoon baking soda

1½ cups old-fashioned rolled oats

½ cup raisins

½ cup chopped pecans (optional)

Preheat the oven to 350°F. Cream the butter, brown sugar, and granulated sugar in a large mixing bowl until light and fluffy. In a small bowl, whisk together the egg and vanilla. Add the egg mixture to the butter mixture and beat until combined.

Sift the flour, cinnamon, cloves, salt, baking powder, and baking soda into a medium bowl. Gradually add the flour mixture to the butter mixture and beat until combined. Stir in the oats, raisins, and pecans, if using. Drop the cookie dough by rounded tablespoons 2 inches apart onto an ungreased baking sheet, flattening the dough slightly by hand.

Bake the cookies for 12 minutes, or until the centers are set. Remove the cookies from the oven and allow them to cool completely before removing them from the baking sheet.

oatmeal raisin cookie ice-cream sandwiches

MAKES 12 SANDWICHES *Here's an ice-cream sandwich with wide appeal—all the goodness of an oatmeal raisin cookie and all the allure of white chocolate and allspice.*

24 Oatmeal-Raisin Cookies (page 46)

1 to 1½ quarts White Chocolate–Allspice Ice Cream (page 23) or your favorite spice cream, slightly softened.

Place one cookie top side down. Scoop ⅓ to ½ cup of ice cream onto the cookie. Place another cookie top side up on the ice cream and press gently to flatten the ice cream between the two cookies. Serve the ice-cream sandwiches immediately.

cardamom snickerdoodle ice-cream sandwiches

MAKES 9 SANDWICHES *A snickerdoodle with a big scoop of ice cream would be a treat in itself. Add spiced bananas to the mix, and this ice-cream sandwich will linger in your memory.*

18 Cardamom
Snickerdoodles (page 50)

3 to 4½ cups Brown Sugar
and Spiced Banana Ice
Cream (page 17) or your
favorite spice cream,
slightly softened.

Place one cookie top side down. Scoop ⅓ to ½ cup of ice cream onto the cookie. Place another cookie top side up on the ice cream and press gently to flatten the ice cream between the two cookies. Serve the ice-cream sandwiches immediately.

cardamom snickerdoodles

· ·

MAKES 1½ DOZEN COOKIES *These gently spiced snickerdoodles are ideal for ice-cream sandwiches—or for munching along with a dish of your favorite spice cream.*

8 tablespoons (1 stick) unsalted butter, at room temperature

¾ cup plus 2 tablespoons sugar

1 egg

½ teaspoon vanilla

1½ cups all-purpose flour

1 teaspoon cream of tartar

1 teaspoon dried lemon zest

½ teaspoon baking soda

⅛ teaspoon salt

1 teaspoon ground cinnamon

1 teaspoon ground cardamom

Preheat the oven to 350°F. Cream the butter and ¾ cup of the sugar in a large mixing bowl until light and fluffy. In a small bowl, whisk together the egg and vanilla. Add the egg mixture to the butter mixture and beat until combined.

Sift the flour, cream of tartar, lemon zest, baking soda, and salt into a medium bowl. Gradually add the flour mixture to the butter mixture and beat until combined.

Mix together the remaining 2 tablespoons of sugar, cinnamon, and cardamom in a small bowl. Scoop the dough by rounded tablespoons and shape the dough into balls. Roll the dough balls in the sugar mixture and place them 2 inches apart on an ungreased baking sheet. Bake the cookies for 13 to 14 minutes, or until the centers are set. Remove the cookies from the oven and allow them to cool completely before removing them from the baking sheet.

chocolate-walnut cookies

MAKES ABOUT 2 DOZEN COOKIES *Here's a yummy cookie for making ice-cream sandwiches. We like the coriander–orange zest combination, but you can substitute orange zest and cloves for a spicier taste.*

1¼ cups plus ¾ cup semisweet chocolate chips

4 tablespoons (½ stick) unsalted butter

⅔ cup sugar

1 egg

2 teaspoons vanilla

⅔ cup all-purpose flour

2 teaspoons dried orange zest

1 teaspoon ground coriander

½ teaspoon baking powder

¼ teaspoon baking soda

¼ teaspoon salt

½ cup chopped walnuts

Preheat the oven to 350°F. Melt 1¼ cups of the chocolate chips and the butter in a double boiler over low heat, stirring often, until smooth. Remove from the heat and set aside to cool. In a large mixing bowl, beat the sugar, egg, and vanilla together. Add the melted chocolate and beat until combined.

Sift the flour, orange zest, coriander, baking powder, baking soda, and salt into a small bowl. Gradually add the flour mixture to the chocolate mixture and beat until combined. Stir in the remaining ¾ cup of chocolate chips and the walnuts. Drop the cookie dough by rounded tablespoons 2 inches apart onto an ungreased baking sheet, flattening slightly by hand. Bake the cookies for 12 minutes, or until the centers are set. Remove the cookies from the oven and allow them to cool completely before removing them from the baking sheet.

chocolate–walnut cookie ice-cream sandwiches

MAKES 12 SANDWICHES *Chocolate and vanilla are two of the world's favorite flavors, particularly in regard to ice cream. Pair them in a luscious, spiced-up ice-cream sandwich and the result is cool perfection.*

12 Chocolate-Walnut Cookies (page 51)

1 to 1½ quarts Vanilla-Cardamom Ice Cream (page 4) or your favorite spice cream, slightly softened.

Place one cookie top side down. Scoop ⅓ to ½ cup of ice cream onto the cookie. Place another cookie top side up on the ice cream and press gently to flatten the ice cream between the two cookies. Serve the ice-cream sandwiches immediately.

peach waffle sundaes with cinnamon syrup

MAKES 4 SUNDAES *Here's a nicely spiced dessert full of delightful flavors. This recipe serves four, but don't be surprised if you get requests for seconds.*

3 to 4 cups White Chocolate–Allspice Ice Cream (page 23) or your favorite spice cream

8 wedges Spiced Pumpkin Dessert Waffles (page 77)

1 cup freshly chopped peaches

¾ cup Cinnamon Syrup (page 69)

½ cup Clove Candied Pecans (page 73), cut into pieces

Scoop the ice cream into 4 separate bowls. Tuck 2 waffle wedges into each bowl of ice cream. Spoon the chopped peaches over the top. Drizzle cinnamon syrup over each sundae and top with pecans. Serve immediately.

caramel apple sundaes

MAKES 4 SUNDAES *If you love caramel apples—and even if you don't—this apple-themed sundae will bring you the joys of caramel sauce wrapped in the satisfaction of true comfort food, with just enough spice to pique your palate.*

3 to 4 cups Spiced Apple Ice Cream (page 13)

1 cup Spiced Caramel Sauce (page 67)

½ cup Clove Candied Pecans (page 73), cut into pieces

Whipped cream, for garnish

4 strawberries, for garnish

Scoop the Spiced Apple Ice Cream into 4 separate bowls. Drizzle the Spiced Caramel Sauce over each sundae and top with pecans. Garnish with whipped cream and a strawberry. Serve immediately.

triple-chocolate sundaes

MAKES 4 SUNDAES *You've heard of "death by chocolate"? We say live well with a chocolate-chocolate-chocolate sundae that will transport you to otherworldly realms of delight.*

3 to 4 cups Dark Chocolate–Anise Ice Cream (page 24)

Chocolate-Walnut Cookies (page 51)

1 cup Spiced Chocolate Sauce (page 68)

Whipped cream, for garnish

4 strawberries, for garnish

Scoop the Dark Chocolate–Anise Ice Cream into 4 separate bowls. Tuck 2 Chocolate-Walnut Cookies into each bowl. Drizzle the Spiced Chocolate Sauce over each sundae. Garnish with whipped cream and a strawberry. Serve immediately.

curried banana splits

MAKES 2 BANANA SPLITS *Curry blends have captivated curious palates for centuries. The curry powder in this recipe works beautifully with the brown sugar, vanilla, and cream to lend a memorable flair to that old favorite, banana splits. This sophisticated dessert will wow your guests and family alike.*

2 tablespoons butter

½ cup firmly packed brown sugar (light or dark)

1 teaspoon curry powder

⅓ cup cream

½ teaspoon vanilla

2 bananas, halved lengthwise

3 cups Coconut-Ginger Sorbet (page 33) or your favorite spice cream

Whipped cream, for garnish

Clove Candied Pecans (page 73), for garnish

Maraschino cherries, for garnish

To make the curried bananas, melt the butter in a large skillet over medium heat. Add the sugar and the curry powder and cook, stirring continually, until the sugar completely dissolves, about 4 minutes. Add the cream and the vanilla and whisk until the sauce is smooth, about 1 minute. Add the bananas and cook, swirling the pan, until the bananas are just heated through, about 1 minute. Do not overcook the bananas.

To assemble the banana splits, place 2 banana halves on opposite sides of a dish. Place 2 to 3 small scoops of Coconut-Curry Sorbet in a row between the banana halves. Spoon ¼ cup of the remaining caramel curry sauce over the sorbet. Top with whipped cream, pecans, and a cherry. Repeat with any remaining ingredients. Serve immediately.

banana split ice-cream cake

MAKES 1 (8-INCH SQUARE) CAKE *Whether you're a fan of banana splits or chocolate cake or fresh takes on old ideas, you'll find plenty to love in this recipe. Perfect for parties or even birthdays, this spectacular cake is a winner.*

6 ounces semisweet chocolate, finely chopped

4 tablespoons (½ stick) unsalted butter

2 eggs

½ cup sugar

1 tablespoon vanilla

¼ teaspoon salt

2 tablespoons all-purpose flour

1 teaspoon ground cinnamon

1 teaspoon ground coriander

3 cups Brown Sugar and Spiced Banana Ice Cream (page 17), slightly softened

Spiced Chocolate Sauce (page 68), for garnish

Zesty Whipped Cream (page 78), for garnish

Clove Candied Pecans (page 73), for garnish

Maraschino cherries, for garnish

Preheat the oven to 300°F. Melt the chocolate and the butter in a double boiler over medium heat, stirring continually, until smooth. In a medium bowl, whisk together the eggs, sugar, vanilla, and salt. Pour the melted chocolate into the egg mixture and whisk until smooth. Add the flour, cinnamon, and coriander and whisk until just combined.

Grease and flour an 8-inch square baking pan. Pour the batter into the pan. Bake the cake for 35 to 40 minutes. Remove the cake from the oven and allow the cake to cool completely.

Spread the ice cream evenly over the cake. Cover the cake and freeze for at least 4 hours or overnight. Remove the cake from the freezer and cut it into squares. Serve each ice-cream cake square topped with chocolate sauce, whipped cream, pecans, and a cherry.

strawberry frozen yogurt parfaits

MAKES 4 PARFAITS *Perfect for starting a full breakfast, finishing a fancy brunch, or any other time, this frozen yogurt parfait fills most any bill. Feel free to vary the yogurt or the crumble. We also love this with lemon-allspice frozen yogurt and really ripe peaches.*

3 cups Strawberry-Cinnamon Frozen Yogurt (page 39), slightly softened

3 cups assorted fresh berries (raspberries, blackberries, blueberries, strawberries)

2 cups Ginger Oat-Nut Crumble (page 71)

In each of 4 footed parfait or ice-cream glasses, scoop ¼ cup of frozen yogurt. On top of the frozen yogurt, layer ¼ cup of berries, ¼ cup of crumble, and ¼ cup of frozen yogurt. Repeat the layering, using ¼ cup each of the berries, crumble, and frozen yogurt. Top each parfait with ¼ cup of the berries and serve immediately.

frozen raspberry cheesecake

MAKES 1 (9-INCH) CHEESECAKE *Surprise your friends, family, and special guests with a dessert that elegantly straddles the line between two irresistible treats—cheesecake and ice cream. Throw in some gentle spices and juicy ripe berries, and watch the slices disappear.*

1½ cups graham cracker crumbs

8 tablespoons (1 stick) butter, melted

3 tablespoons sugar

1 teaspoon ground coriander

1 quart Cinnamon-Raspberry Cheesecake Ice Cream (page 22)

Zesty Whipped Cream (page 78), for garnish

Preheat the oven to 350°F. Mix the graham cracker crumbs, butter, sugar, and coriander in a small bowl. Press the crust mixture into the bottom of a 9-inch springform pan. Bake for 6 to 8 minutes; cool completely.

Fill the cooled graham cracker crust with the raspberry cheesecake ice cream, softening it slightly first, if necessary. Place the cake in the freezer for at least 4 hours before serving.

Serve slices of cheesecake garnished with the zesty whipped cream.

spice cream milkshakes

MAKES 4 MILKSHAKES *Milkshakes make the world go 'round. At least we're tempted to think so every time we sip the real thing. If a plain milkshake is that good, just imagine how delicious one can be when you add some spice. How about a Cardamom-Mint Ice Cream milkshake, or a Brown Sugar and Spiced Banana Ice Cream milkshake? And do try Dark Chocolate–Anise Ice Cream with chocolate milk. The possibilities are endless.*

4 cups of your favorite spice cream

2 cups milk

1 teaspoon vanilla (optional)

Place the spice cream, milk, and vanilla in a blender. Blend the shakes until thoroughly combined and smooth. Serve immediately.

root beer floats

MAKES 4 ROOT BEER FLOATS *Once you discover the fun of spicing things up, it's fun to do so with all those other ice-cream treats. What could be simpler, or more iconic, than an ice-cream float? This one calls for root beer, but feel free to substitute your favorite soda or other beverage. We're partial to spiced chocolate ice cream—maybe Dark Chocolate–Anise (page 24) with Yoo-hoo, our favorite bottled chocolate beverage.*

1 quart Vanilla-Cardamom Ice Cream (page 4) or your favorite spice cream

4 bottles very cold old-fashioned root beer

Whipped cream, for garnish

In each of 4 footed fountain glasses or mugs, scoop 1 cup of the ice cream. Slowly pour the root beer over the ice cream. Top with whipped cream and serve immediately with a straw and long-handled spoon.

Candied Pecan
Meringue Shells
(page 76)

Ice cream is delicious all on its own, but it's also a perfect vehicle for embellishments. In fact, if there's one thing better than a big serving of ice cream, it's an ice-cream sundae, or an ice-cream sandwich, or maybe a milkshake or float.

Part of the fun of making ice cream is dressing it up, and mixing and matching it with cookies for sandwiches or various syrups for a new twist on a sundae. This chapter gives you plenty of extras to work with, from cinnamon syrup to a fabulous, spiced-up chocolate sauce, and from spiced nuts to crumbly toppings you'll want to add to many of your favorite treats.

We hope you will try these recipes, then use your imagination to vary them any way you like, and to mix and match them with various ice creams or sorbets.

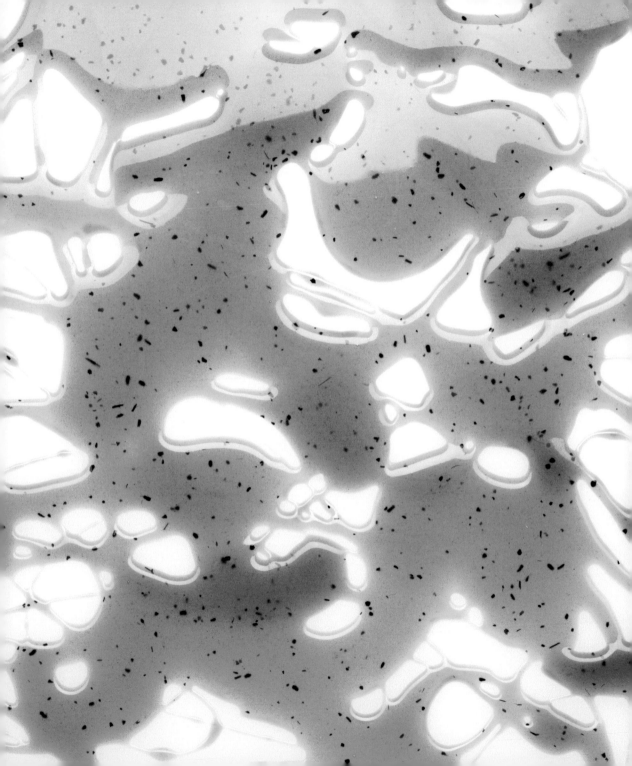

spiced caramel sauce

MAKES 2 CUPS *You thought caramel sauce couldn't get better? Try it with cloves and see what you've been missing. Feel free to substitute cardamom, cinnamon, or another spice for the cloves.*

1 cup heavy cream

1¼ cups firmly packed brown sugar (light or dark)

1 teaspoon ground cloves

4 tablespoons (½ stick) butter

1 teaspoon vanilla

Bring the cream to a boil in a small saucepan over medium heat. Add the brown sugar and the cloves and cook, stirring continually, until the sugar dissolves, about 5 minutes. Remove the saucepan from the heat and whisk in the butter 1 tablespoon at a time. Stir in the vanilla and serve immediately.

spiced chocolate sauce

MAKES ABOUT 2 CUPS *A plain version of this sauce was sacrosanct in Katie's childhood kitchen. Her brothers ate it for breakfast, especially after Thanksgiving when it could douse a slice of pecan pie and a side of ice cream. The sauce stayed on the counter in a little brown earthenware jug that was as humble looking as the chocolate inside was divine.*

When she serves it now, people who previously claimed an immunity to chocolate's siren song have been caught with their fingers in the pot, licking the concoction with abandon.

This version, with cinnamon and allspice, pairs chocolaty goodness with the sweet tingle of two favorite spices. Master this recipe, and you'll be able to vary it with any spice you like.

For a delicious variation substitute a teaspoon of cumin for the allspice in this recipe.

8 tablespoons (1 stick) unsalted butter

1 cup sugar

½ cup unsweetened cocoa powder

1 teaspoon ground allspice

1 teaspoon ground cinnamon

1 teaspoon salt

½ cup milk or cream

4 ounces semisweet or milk chocolate, finely chopped

1 teaspoon vanilla

Melt the butter in a small saucepan over low heat. Add the sugar and whisk until the sugar begins to dissolve. Add the cocoa powder, allspice, cinnamon, and salt and whisk until smooth. Increase the heat to medium and add the milk, whisking constantly, until the sauce just comes to a boil. Decrease the heat to low and let cook, without stirring, for 2 minutes. Remove the pan from the heat, add the chocolate, and whisk until the chocolate melts and the sauce is smooth. Stir in the vanilla. Serve the chocolate sauce warm or at room temperature.

cinnamon syrup

MAKES ¾ CUP *Master this syrup and you'll have a ready repertoire of enticing toppings—and not just for your favorite ice cream. This recipe features cinnamon, but you can create plenty of variations by substituting a teaspoon of your favorite spice.*

1 cup sugar

¼ cup plus ⅓ cup water

1 teaspoon ground cinnamon

½ teaspoon vanilla

Pinch of salt

Combine the sugar and ¼ cup of the water in a medium, heavy saucepan. Heat the sugar mixture over medium heat, stirring gently, until the sugar has completely dissolved and the syrup is clear; do not boil the mixture until the sugar has completely dissolved. Increase the heat to high, cover the saucepan, and boil the syrup for 2 minutes.

Uncover the saucepan and continue to boil, stirring gently, until the syrup turns a golden bronze, about 3 minutes.

Remove the saucepan from the heat and, standing back, carefully add the remaining ⅓ cup of water. Whisk the syrup until smooth. Add the cinnamon, vanilla, and salt and continue to whisk until the syrup is smooth. Strain the syrup through a fine-mesh sieve.

Serve the syrup immediately. You can also let it cool completely and store it in an airtight container in the refrigerator. Reheat over low heat before serving.

ancho-lime syrup

MAKES ABOUT 1 CUP *This zesty syrup has the perfect kick. It's terrific served over Mango Sorbet with Cumin and Cinnamon (page 35) garnished with a lime twist, but you'll find plenty of other uses for it, too.*

1 cup sugar

¼ cup water

⅓ cup freshly squeezed lime juice

1 teaspoon ground ancho chile

Pinch of salt

Combine the sugar and the water in a medium, heavy saucepan. Heat the sugar mixture over medium heat, stirring gently, until the sugar has completely dissolved and the syrup is clear; do not boil the mixture until the sugar has completely dissolved. Increase the heat to high, cover the saucepan, and boil the syrup for 2 minutes.

Remove the saucepan from the heat and, standing back, carefully add the lime juice. Whisk the syrup until smooth. Add the ancho chile and the salt and continue to whisk until the syrup is smooth. Strain the syrup through a fine-mesh sieve.

Serve the syrup immediately. You can also let it cool completely and store it in an airtight container in the refrigerator. Reheat over low heat before serving.

ginger oat-nut crumble

MAKES 3 CUPS *This granola-like topping is full of good things—good for you but also good to eat. It's a tasty topping for ice cream and frozen yogurt.*

¼ cup firmly packed brown sugar (light or dark)

4 tablespoons (½ stick) unsalted butter

1 teaspoon ground ginger

1 teaspoon ground cinnamon

1 teaspoon dried lemon zest

1 teaspoon vanilla

½ teaspoon salt

1 cup old-fashioned rolled oats

½ cup slivered almonds

½ cup chopped pecans

Preheat the oven to 350°F. Combine the brown sugar, butter, ginger, cinnamon, lemon zest, vanilla, and salt in a small saucepan. Heat the mixture over medium heat, stirring frequently, until the sugar has dissolved.

Combine the oats, almonds, and pecans in a large bowl. Add the brown sugar mixture and toss until the oat and nut mixture is evenly coated. Spread the mixture in a single layer on a jelly roll pan. Bake for 10 to 15 minutes, stirring every 5 minutes. Remove the oat-nut crumble from the oven and allow it to cool before serving. Store in an airtight container for up to 2 weeks, or 4 to 6 weeks in the refrigerator.

clove candied pecans

MAKES 3 CUPS *Cloves and cinnamon turn those nuts into a spicy delight. Be careful not to eat them all as soon as they're cool, or else double the recipe. You'll need them for Pecan Spice Ice Cream (page 11), toppings for sundaes, and more.*

1 egg white

¼ cup sugar

1 teaspoon ground cinnamon

1 teaspoon ground cloves

3 cups pecan halves

Preheat the oven to 350°F. Whisk together the egg white, sugar, cinnamon, and cloves in a small bowl. Pour the egg mixture into a large resealable plastic bag. Add the pecans, seal the bag, and shake until the pecans are evenly coated.

Grease a jelly roll pan. Spread the pecans in a single layer and bake for 10 minutes, stirring halfway through baking. Remove the pan from the oven, loosen the pecans, and let them cool for 10 minutes. Store the pecans in an airtight container for up to 2 weeks, or 4 to 6 weeks in the refrigerator.

cardamom-coconut toasted topping

MAKES 1 CUP *Katie's daughter Diana is a teenager with a sophisticated palate, and this topping is proof. Diana came up with this mixture because she wanted something to sprinkle on a coconut ice cream. It's delicious with sorbets made from coconut milk, but it's also terrific on just about any kind of ice cream.*

½ cup sweetened flaked coconut

½ cup sliced almonds

2 teaspoons fennel seed

1 teaspoon ground cardamom

1 teaspoon ground ginger

Preheat the oven to 350°F. Mix together all the ingredients in a small bowl. Spread the mixture in a single layer on a parchment-lined jelly roll pan. Toast the mixture in the oven, stirring occasionally, until evenly toasted and golden, about 7 minutes. Remove the toasted topping from the oven. Serve warm or at room temperature on top of your favorite spice cream. Store the cooled topping in an airtight container for up to 2 weeks, or 4 to 6 weeks in the refrigerator.

spiced ice-cream cones and bowls

MAKES 9 ICE-CREAM CONES OR BOWLS *Create your own variations of spiced cones and crusty bowls by substituting a teaspoon of your favorite spice. The batter can be made a day ahead and kept in the refrigerator, but the cones and bowls are best eaten the day they are baked.*

1 egg

1 egg white

½ cup sugar

1 teaspoon vanilla

1 teaspoon ground cardamom

⅛ teaspoon salt

⅔ cup all-purpose flour

2 tablespoons unsalted butter, melted and cooled

Preheat the oven to 350°F. Beat together the egg, egg white, sugar, vanilla, cardamom, and salt in a small mixing bowl. Add the flour and beat until just combined. Add the butter and whisk until the batter is smooth.

Spoon 2 level tablespoons of the batter onto a large, parchment-lined baking sheet and use a spoon or small offset spatula to evenly spread the batter into a 6-inch circle. Repeat, using 2 more tablespoons of batter. There should be room to form 2 circles per baking sheet.

Bake the batter until it is evenly light golden brown in color, about 12 minutes. Remove from the oven and quickly loosen with a thin spatula. Immediately shape each circle around a cone-rolling form, pressing the seam firmly and pinching the end to seal the cone, or place each circle over a teacup to form a bowl. You have to work fast, as the cones cool very quickly.

candied pecan meringue shells

MAKES 8 MERINGUE SHELLS *What do you do with all the egg whites left over from making ice cream? That's simple—make meringues! For an elegant dessert, fill these shells with your favorite spice cream and drizzle with ¼ cup of Cinnamon Syrup (page 69) or Spiced Chocolate Sauce (page 68).*

4 large egg whites

½ teaspoon vanilla

½ teaspoon cream of tartar

⅛ teaspoon salt

¾ cup sugar

⅓ cup confectioners' sugar

1 teaspoon ground cinnamon

1 cup Clove Candied Pecans, finely chopped (page 73)

Allow the egg whites to stand at room temperature for 30 minutes.

Preheat the oven to 225°F. Beat together the egg whites, vanilla, cream of tartar, and salt in a large bowl with a mixer on medium speed until the egg whites begin to hold their shape and soft peaks form. Beating on high speed, gradually add the sugar, 1 tablespoon at a time, until stiff peaks form. Sift the confectioners' sugar and the cinnamon together over the meringue and carefully fold it in with a rubber spatula. Gently fold the pecans into the meringue.

Divide the meringue into 8 equal portions and drop the portions 3 inches apart (3 down each side and 2 along the middle) onto a large, parchment-lined baking sheet. Spread the meringue into 3-inch circles and, using the back of a spoon, hollow out the center of each meringue, making a nest in each one.

Bake the meringue shells for 1½ hours. Turn off the oven and let the meringues dry in the oven with the door closed for 1 hour. Remove from the oven and let cool completely. If not using them immediately, store the meringue shells in an airtight container for up to 1 week.

spiced pumpkin dessert waffles

MAKES 2 CUPS OF BATTER *Serve these spiced pumpkin waffles with your favorite spice cream to transform this breakfast staple into an impressive dessert.*

¾ cup all-purpose flour

1½ teaspoons baking powder

¼ teaspoon baking soda

2 teaspoons ground cinnamon

1 teaspoon ground allspice

⅛ teaspoon salt

1 egg, separated

2 tablespoons unsalted butter, melted and cooled

1 tablespoon vanilla

¾ cup milk

½ cup canned pure pumpkin

3 tablespoons firmly packed brown sugar (light or dark)

Preheat a waffle iron. Sift together the flour, baking powder, baking soda, cinnamon, allspice, and salt into a medium mixing bowl. In a small bowl, whisk together the egg yolk, butter, and vanilla until thoroughly combined. Whisk the milk, pumpkin, and brown sugar into the egg mixture until smooth. Add the egg mixture to the flour mixture and stir until just combined.

In a separate bowl, beat the remaining egg white until soft peaks form. Fold the egg white into the pumpkin batter. Coat the waffle iron with nonstick cooking spray or brush it with a flavorless oil (such as canola oil). Pour enough batter in the iron to just cover the waffle grid, close, and cook according to the manufacturer's instructions until golden brown. Remove the waffle and repeat until all the batter is used. Serve the waffles immediately. Extra waffles can be frozen and then reheated in a toaster oven on low heat.

zesty whipped cream

MAKES 2 TO 2½ CUPS *Whipped cream is the crowning glory of plenty of sweet treats. We like ours zesty, but any spice will do. Feel free to substitute a teaspoon of cinnamon, allspice, or other spice for the zest. When it comes to choosing a flavor, we have a simple rule: Suit yourself.*

1 cup cold heavy whipping cream

¼ cup sifted confectioners' sugar

1 teaspoon dried lemon zest

½ teaspoon vanilla

Beat the cream with a mixer on medium speed in a chilled mixing bowl with chilled beaters until thickened. Stir in the sugar, lemon zest, and vanilla and continue beating on medium speed until soft peaks form. Perfectly whipped cream should be billowy and stiff but still smooth. Serve the whipped cream immediately.

metric conversion formulas

to convert	multiply
Ounces to grams	Ounces by 28.35
Pounds to kilograms	Pounds by 0.454
Teaspoons to milliliters	Teaspoons by 4.93
Tablespoons to milliliters	Tablespoons by 14.79
Fluid ounces to milliliters	Fluid ounces by 29.57
Cups to milliliters	Cups by 236.59
Cups to liters	Cups by 0.236
Pints to liters	Pints by 0.473
Quarts to liters	Quarts by 0.946
Gallons to liters	Gallons by 3.785
Inches to centimeters	Inches by 2.54

approximate metric equivalents

volume

¼ teaspoon	1 milliliter
½ teaspoon	2.5 milliliters
¾ teaspoon	4 milliliters
1 teaspoon	5 milliliters
1¼ teaspoons	6 milliliters
1½ teaspoons	7.5 milliliters
1¾ teaspoons	8.5 milliliters
2 teaspoons	10 milliliters
1 tablespoon (½ fluid ounce)	15 milliliters
2 tablespoons (1 fluid ounce)	30 milliliters
¼ cup	60 milliliters
⅓ cup	80 milliliters
½ cup (4 fluid ounces)	120 milliliters
⅔ cup	160 milliliters
¾ cup	180 milliliters
1 cup (8 fluid ounces)	240 milliliters
1¼ cups	300 milliliters
1½ cups (12 fluid ounces)	360 milliliters

1⅔ cups   400 milliliters
2 cups (1 pint)   460 milliliters
3 cups   700 milliliters
4 cups (1 quart)   0.95 liter
1 quart plus ¼ cup   1 liter
4 quarts (1 gallon)   3.8 liters

weight
¼ ounce   7 grams
½ ounce   14 grams
¾ ounce   21 grams
1 ounce   28 grams
1¼ ounces   35 grams
1½ ounces   42.5 grams
1⅔ ounces   45 grams
2 ounces   57 grams
3 ounces   85 grams
4 ounces (¼ pound)   113 grams
5 ounces   142 grams
6 ounces   170 grams
7 ounces   198 grams
8 ounces (½ pound)   227 grams
16 ounces (1 pound)   454 grams
35.25 ounces (2.2 pounds)   1 kilogram

length
⅛ inch   3 millimeters
¼ inch   6 millimeters
½ inch   1.25 centimeters
1 inch   2.5 centimeters
2 inches   5 centimeters
2½ inches   6 centimeters
4 inches   10 centimeters
5 inches   13 centimeters
6 inches   15.25 centimeters
12 inches (1 foot)   30 centimeters

oven temperatures

To convert Fahrenheit to Celsius, subtract 32 from Fahrenheit, multiply the result by 5, then divide by 9.

description	fahrenheit	celsius	british gas mark
Very cool	200°	95°	0
Very cool	225°	110°	¼
Very cool	250°	120°	½
Cool	275°	135°	1
Cool	300°	150°	2
Warm	325°	165°	3
Moderate	350°	175°	4
Moderately hot	375°	190°	5
Fairly hot	400°	200°	6
Hot	425°	220°	7
Very hot	450°	230°	8
Very hot	475°	245°	9

common ingredients and their approximate equivalents

1 cup uncooked rice = 225 grams
1 cup all-purpose flour = 140 grams
1 stick butter (4 ounces • ½ cup • 8 tablespoons) = 110 grams
1 cup butter (8 ounces • 2 sticks • 16 tablespoons) = 220 grams
1 cup brown sugar, firmly packed = 225 grams
1 cup granulated sugar = 200 grams

Information compiled from a variety of sources, including *Recipes into Type* by Joan Whitman and Dolores Simon (Newton, MA: Biscuit Books, 2000); *The New Food Lover's Companion* by Sharon Tyler Herbst (Hauppauge, NY: Barron's, 1995); and *Rosemary Brown's Big Kitchen Instruction Book* (Kansas City, MO: Andrews McMeel, 1998).

index